Shortlisted for the Bare Fiction Debut Poetry Collection Competition in 2015 and a winner in the Terry Hetherington Award for Young Writers in 2016, Christina Thatcher's poetry and short stories have featured in a number of publications including *The London Magazine*, *Planet Magazine*, *Acumen* and *The Interpreter's House*.

Thatcher grew up in America but has made a happy home in Wales with her husband, Rich, and cat, Miso. She is a PhD student and postgraduate tutor at Cardiff University where she studies how creative writing can impact the lives of people bereaved by addiction. Thatcher keeps busy off campus too by delivering creative writing workshops across south Wales, running projects for organisations including Making Minds and the Welsh Writers' Trust and coordinating literature events for the Made in Roath Festival.

To learn more about Thatcher's work visit her website: https://christinathatcher.com or follow her on Twitter: @writetoempower.

More than you were

Christina Thatcher

Parthian, Cardigan SA43 1ED www.parthianbooks.com
First published in 2017
© Christina Thatcher 2017
ISBN 978-1-912109-70-8
Editor: Susie Wild
Cover design by Torben Schacht
Typeset by Elaine Sharples
Printed in EU by Pulsio SARL
Published with the financial support of the Welsh Books Council British
Library Cataloguing in Publication Data
A cataloguing record for this book is available from the British Library.

Contents

First Drafts

By the time I wrote your obituary
I had read hundreds of them,
searching for words to flesh you out;
you did so little with your life.
The first lines were just facts—
your age, the names of your children
when and where you died.
Later I wrote that you were kind,
deep down. I thought I owed that to you,
the way a mother owes it to her son
to dress him well for his school photo.
I didn't want you to look bad
next to the other obituaries.

Day One

My mother breaks
the news through high-pitched
sobs and errant curses. She calls you
Daddy – your death makes me a child again.
The phone is heavy, becomes heavier,
as I flick in and out of the conversation.
I think I must be practical, must listen,
must do things. But I don't.
I just stay still as the room
moves in, slow and cool,
like molasses.

Lesson #1

The day she severed
the head of a snake
with the toy shovel
I used in the garden
she turned to me
and said – quiet and strong –
that in order to protect
our family we must sometimes
do unfair and gruesome things.

When days were longer

In the kitchen my grandmother sings
half-remembered hymns from Sunday service.
Oh Father, bring me peace.
Oh Jesus, lay me down.

She makes crescent cookies
filled with almonds and thanks
the Lord we're not
allergic.

On the stove the sugar burns—
but she doesn't seem to notice.
Instead, she hums, chops nuts, sways her hips
as I watch and listen, from the floor.

There

I remember you
singing in the kitchen
your father built, laying
pasta down in sheets,
stirring sauces, white and red,
in time with your rhythm: blues.

It was all so ordinary—
your cracking voice,
the overflowing trash can,
bags of dog food,
yellow linoleum.

You were everything in that room—
the expert, alchemist, front man
composing lasagna
I will never taste
again.

Full

The morning after you died
I woke up to hot chili, eggs and soup.
He told me he'd made all three meals
for the day – didn't know when or what
I'd like to eat. I stood in the kitchen,
stared at the pots – the room still warm,
full of smells – and thought how much
I'd wanted you to look after me this way,
giving me all the things I needed to grow.

Lesson #2

You told me
with one swift movement
like spiders on a pillow,
never to touch fire—
your fingers will blister,
you said, and young girls
are only ever as good
as their skin.

Anticipation

I sat in the car
and waited
for whatever
you were doing
to finish.

You told me
if I was good
I could have
my own pack
of red gum
from the store.

For hours
I imagined
the taste
of cinnamon
that never came.

Brushing Teeth

As a child I heard that toothpaste
was made from the bodies of dead
sea creatures. Tiny things. Cretaceous.

This knowledge brought me closer
to the sea. And with it, my life began
to erode in the mornings and at night:

the sink became a whale's mouth,
gaping, expectant. The *swish swish*
of bristles and foam turned to waves

lapping and tidal against my cheeks.
My wooden footstool played the boat,
rickety yet smooth beneath my toes.

And with every Captain's spit and jaunty rinse
I moved inland again, slowly,
back to shore.

Searching

On nights when your screams
made it too hard to sleep
I'd slip out my window,
feet on concrete, and climb
up the pine in the yard,
looking out hard for some place
farther than I was able to see.

Keeping Up

The week after you die I fall,
elbows first, on the cold floor
of a Cardiff car park—
I am running from zombies.

It is supposed to be fun,
my friends are laughing
dressed like film stars,

but I fall,

hit the ground so hard
that even the zombies back away.

I know that it is over—
realize I can only run for so long,
can only pick gravel from my skin,
watch the ambulance man bandage my arm,
before I, too, will be taken
to the place you are now.

The Only Time

I still feel the thud—
the sudden *whoosh*
my body made
as it was flung
over the couch.
Still notice the pain
along the back
of my neck, pinched
between the thick folds
of your fingers. But most of all,
I still hear the sound
of your voice, guttural
and slurred, reminding me
that if I ever left home
again it would be worse,
next time.

The Talk

You didn't expect it to happen
so fast, the packing, the moving on.
You told me not to go, that I'd always
belong there. You told a story
about your father, how old he was,
how he died. You drank your beer
as I sat, stiff and quiet on the bed,
wishing this talk had come sooner.

Men in Our Family Die Early

He lasted 17 years longer
than his own father
who died in mysterious
circumstances after the war.

You're lucky I'm not like my dad,
he'd say. I don't use a willow
switch, don't beat you red raw
after church.

It's true, he was better than his dad—

his body making impressions only
on thick sofa cushions, his fingers
on the curves of our tiny necks.

Before he died his hands taught us
never to fight back, never to swear,
always to think of the cur.

Silo

As children we dared each other
to climb inside— birds cooed at the top,
flapped their wings, left the walls
sticky and feathered. I imagined
what it was like during the dairy farm days
bursting with sweet grain and oats,
pictured my grandfather shoveling it out
after the cows had gone and the horses came—
experienced the empty space for myself years later,
legs pulled up tight, ears blocked,
until the cold, echoing tin forced
me out, reminding me there
were so few places
I could go.

Enabling

You burned down our house
hours after I turned 21.
The next day, when all
the silt had been pumped
from the pond, I drove you
to the pharmacy— past the old
Burger King and stray dog alley—
so you could get what you needed
to forget what you'd done.

In the backyard

It was comical, the feud.
Dad throwing cans of Budweiser
over the fence, the neighbors
hurling trash and blasting music.
It was all Elmer Fudd and Bugs Bunny,
silly and mischievous, until the night
we heard squawking, loud and manic
from our chicken coop. We woke up,
my brother and I, to the crashing of wire.
Shining a light out the window we saw him—
the dog, their dog, no collar, eyes gleaming
wild, fur full of feathers and blood.

Lesson #3

He asked me to wait
by the window and watch
as he slit the throat
of my pet turkey.
I saw the whole thing—
its head bobbing,
the blood splattering,
my sobs fogging
up the glass. Later,
to comfort me, he said
that some things were
never meant to be loved.

The Toxicologist

Weeks after your death,
after your ashes were funneled
into plastic bags to share out
among the family, the toxicologist
called to say that it wasn't just cocaine.
He listed it all – his voice soft,
Southern, uneasy. I could tell
he'd dreaded this call. So I listened,
said I knew how it would end.
This made it easier for him,
to know that I knew
what you had done.

Grief

I am the centerpiece,
a quiet bird that everything
is meant to happen around.
I am expected to stay still,
to listen, to receive and repeat platitudes—
not be too emotional. I must be sad
but not too sad. Not hysterically sad.
Still I flutter and feel things.
My emotions swell up, squawking.
I flap my wings, become unpredictable.
I make unbeautiful sounds.
People hurtle towards me
as I try and fail to break free.

Choices

In the cool, low-lit office
of the funeral director
I was told to choose an urn—
one that I would like
or one that he would like.

They were polished,
placed on spot-lit shelves
like diamonds in a strip mall.

With two men towering behind me,
their next appointment knocking,
I selected something silver
with a Celtic pattern

because once Dad told me
he had the skin of an Irishman,
that turned red as boiled lobsters
from our kitchen pot.

Shaking hands at a funeral

He said that death would strip me—
leave me barren, like winter,
standing in the cold.
He said that my body
would mean something different
from now on. That my skin
would change and soon
I would no longer see
my father in my face.

Multiples

She will attend her fifth funeral
this month. It's the fourth family member,
the other was a friend from a long time ago.
I watch her eating chicken,
talking slow and flat in between.
It must get easier, I told her,
make you stronger. No, she said,
that's wrong. A little piece of me
dies with every death. Soon, she told me—
ketchup staining the corners of her mouth—
I'll be dead too.

Incarnation

She said there must be a link
between feathers and fathers—
told me she'd plucked
a slim one from her hair
the day after her father hung
himself. It was brown with flecks
of white, from a pigeon
on Albany Road. It was him,
she assured me. He always liked
to make an entrance.

Needs

I cannot help but seek out
other people's grief. Home in on it,
ask probing, inappropriate questions.

In walking distance from my house—
the one I said we might be buying,
with the Welsh slate and the stained glass
window of a church— there are three suicides,
two cancers, one brain hemorrhage. All fathers.

I listen to their stories for relief, tell mine
to keep from going mad.

Etiquette

I knew when you died
I would no longer be good
at dinner parties.
My friends laughed about it.
I stopped caring for pleasant things.
Forget the weather, budding
careers, teething children.
Tell me about your trauma,
the nights when you can't sleep.
Tell me when you've failed—
clipped like a deer in the forest.
Tell me things you never wanted
to tell anyone. Only the worst
will sate me now.

Lesson #4

After we bumped into
my crush in the market
she clasped my arm
and said, if you ever
have sex with that boy
God will leave you—
swift and cold—
like a ship swept
under the sea.

Learning from our father

My brother comes in handcuffs
to our father's funeral. Two officers
sit in the corner as we hug
like T-Rexes in front of the urn.
He shuffles around the room in clothes
I picked out— a blue and yellow polo,
white khaki trousers, black shoes
one size too small. He stops
at the collages, pointing to pictures
of Dad taken long before we were born,
then asks how soon it will be before
he's back here being looked at, whispered about—
just photos glued to cheap cardboard.

Terminology

In the months that followed
I would learn the terminology
of grief. Read outpourings on blogs,
collect informational leaflets,
buy more than one book with
a woman crying on the cover.
I would study it. Turn it over
and over, will it to move
to the mind and no longer
bubble up from the gut
– searing and heavy –
like tar.

The things we say

I gave my speech and hours later,
in a bar where I stepped in gum,
my Mom played a voicemail
left by one of his friends.

He said what I shared was profound—
that I was brave, articulate
and surprising. And I said,
scraping my shoe against
the leg of my stool,

it's a pity that Dad
couldn't hear it.

Knowing

She told me the dog knew
what had happened and why—
said the night your father
chased me with that iron poker
from the fire, stuck it right against
my throat the dog knew that soon
he would die. Bad men always die.
Now that he's gone the dog sleeps
easier in the bed next to me.

Something else

The squirrels are coming
my uncle said, that's what I call
the neighbors. They came
swift and chattering within minutes
to tell me what my father looked like
when they found him— a blowfish on the bed.
She said she had a miscarriage
but hoped for another child—
my dad bought her a wedding dress,
tucked away in the closet ready
for when she stopped drinking.
Standing next to a pile of dog shit
she asked me for money. I was the cleaner
she said. I cleaned the house.

Clearing Out

Receipts mix with razorblades
in the top drawer of his desk.
A photo of a woman, Eastern European,
stares up from an open manila folder.
She's kneeling down in a hotel lobby
next to a plant with thick, waxy leaves.
Her fingers clasp its bulky stalk
as she smiles back at the camera,
directly. Underneath the photos
lies her passport, Romanian.
And plane tickets, from Cairo.
He was never good with geography.
There are bank statements too.
She cleared him out. And yet he still believed,
until the end, that she would come.

Hollow

I can see his innards now
exposed in empty pill bottles
rolling across his nightstand.
Razorblades and magnum condoms
scattered around his desk. Blood
smeared on the corners of white tiles.

I can hear his heartbeat here.
An old sleep apnea machine
humming next to his bed frame.
A thick cane knocking against the wall—
hung up next to his leather jacket
by the door.

I can see inside him, deep,
but everything looks hollow now.

The Couch

I imagine you there—
sinking into fabric
too thick for the Florida heat.
In my mind you are drinking beer,
calling out to the neighbors
with nicknames you've given them,
petting a dog you should never
have gotten. You have nothing
to do but this   sit, sweating
on the couch until, weeks after
you've gone, I see the imprint
of your body and think
of where you've been.

Guide

He asked for a tour,
the neighbor with the Corona—
claimed your house was the biggest
in the complex. I stared at him and said,
I am the daughter not the realtor.
C'mon, just a quick look. I sighed,
led him to your bedroom past the blood stains,
the sacks of steaming garbage. He whistled,
took a swig of beer, was impressed.
Your death didn't bother him at all.

My room in your house

I never thought it would be like this—
the white and blue paint, the faint smell
of gasoline, the windowsill still cluttered
with dead dragonflies. I never imagined
the single bed made carefully with
yellowed sheets, a loaded gun left
under the mattress. I never expected
the fear that came, quick and chaotic,
when I opened the door, or the lump
that moved hard to my throat
when you told me once that I
belonged there.

Reoccurring

For months I dream
that you are holding me down—
pinning me to the back seat of cars,
trapping me against cold, bathroom tiles.
I watch the needle, hear you soothing:
this will make you feel better,
this will make you feel better,
before squeezing my eyes shut,
willing my pupils to stay small
my body to keep calm, concentrate,
freeze the veins, so I don't let you in,
feel your mistakes lurch
through my blood.

Safeguard

I see faces in the night

peering through windows
behind cupboard doors.

Sometimes they look like you,
other times they resemble

the drug addict living in our patio
who peeped at me in the shower,

the old man in our basement
who smiled while shooting up,

the biker who touched my thigh
when I was ten.

All the men who lurched forward
into my young life and   hovered there,

invited in by the one
who was meant to protect me.

Change

The smell of wet dog, sour milk
and damp clothes reminds me of you.
This never used to be your smell.
But now I can't remember when
the scent you used to carry—
cut grass and engine grease—
turned stale. I only know that it did, slowly,
until you reeked of someone else.

Sealed

I sign the paperwork
which states that someone
else will own your house—
take possession of the fleas,
the blood-stained floors,
the cans of old tomatoes.
I don't think anyone has told
the new owners that more
than one person has died there.
I imagine them making friends
with the neighbors, drinking
warm cans of Budweiser,
sweating in the Florida heat—
bodies puffed up like pastry.
I picture them waiting for something,
anything, to happen before they too
are carried out by hazmat men
from the space where your bed
used to be.

Lesson #5

We spent our summers
sweating on the farm
until the day he threw
dynamite into the creek.
This will kill the eels,
he told us, never say
I don't do enough
for you again.

Sharing

Deciding where to spread your ashes
I consider the things you'd love about Wales—

fishing in the River Taff, walking along
Rhossili, laying on Langland beach.

I want you to enjoy yourself, to see
the things I've seen. I want you

to be better somehow, more
attentive, than you were before.

Old Habits

I consider keeping
you closer to home,
spreading your ashes thin
across the garden,
yet can't help but think
you will make your way
to the back alley – sell pills
to the boy next door.
After all, he's good and kind
and foolish and you
just can't help yourself,
even now.

Black Hole

Your voice rung through the house
like reverberating metal: *I made you*
so I can take you away. The words
were truest when you murdered
the hermit crabs — smashed their glass
cage on the drive, and when you bloodied
your hands against my door, my brother's
face, or other hard, persistent objects.
It was those times I believed you.
But now, just ashes, I never imagined
you would take me. Never thought you'd
rip a hole so big it could suck my life right out.

Ordinary Things

I'm reading poetry on the train—
and, as the morning slips by,
blue and fleeting, you find me.

I crumple my sandwich wrapper
to drown the roar of your laugh,
the sight of your beer belly, the smell
of a piss-stained carpet. I gulp

some water and remember
your Adam's apple, how it bulged out
of your neck before I moved away.

I scan the seats and want
to be like the other passengers,
want everything to be quiet
and easy again.

Repeat

Through glassy eyes he tells me
he hates the food in England.
He visited Blackpool once,
in the 90s, worked in a factory
where he sold a pair of Levis
to a man without any shoes.
I'd heard this story many times
but still, I smiled and listened—
never thinking this would be
the last time I'd hear that the pub
was fucking miles away.

M55

I pass the sign for Blackpool
and suddenly my seat becomes
your seat. I look closer, imagine
this is the first time I have seen
English hills, smelt the damp air,
heard plays being read on Radio 4.

I picture you opening your passport
again and again to show off
your new photo to the van driver—
work had paid for it all.

By now, after hours of travel,
boots heavy, you would be planning
what to say to the other men
on the production line.

Here, far from your family,
you could be anyone: a horse tamer,
pool shark, country singer,
the frozen food factory king.

Here, no one could see
the life you led
back home.

Out

I wonder if he liked
dining alone. While I grew,
he stayed late in restaurants
buying drinks for strangers,
telling stories. It must have
made him feel powerful—
to create the family
he wanted with just words
and bottles of Bud.

Lesson #6

He came with me
the first time but
didn't help at all.
Instead, he laughed.
Turned to the pharmacist
and joked he could never
trust someone who bled
for seven days and didn't die.

Back to Work

I push through deadlines, daily admin, late nights,
work hard and steady, my head still pounding
with pictures of you—

the green bean bowl, overheated,
exploding in your hands, our matching
seabass T-shirts, that low-slung belt.

No matter how much typing I do I can only think
of your slopped frame, the way you moved,
a father's body.

I do the things I need to do but dully, with effort,
as though I'm wading through wet sand or wrapped,
head to toe, in cellophane.

Numb

The butterflies died with him—
my stomach settled as if it knew
nothing could disturb it more
than that plane ride, the first glimpse
of his house, the smell of stale alcohol,
dead birds. My knees don't shake
any more with fear or excitement.
I squeeze them, daily, under my desk
to make sure they can still feel
anything at all.

Playing Nice

When the therapist told me
to create my own metaphor for grief—
to represent it as a tall mountain
or grains of sand trickling into a jar—
I could only think of machetes.
Could only remember the man
who collected them in Philly
and chased children down the street—
wild, unpredictable, violent. I knew
this woman would not approve,
did not want my metaphor to be
a lurching, sweat-soaked man.
Instead I told her that my grief
was a river, boxed in by an ailing city,
making its way slow and heavy
to the sea.

The Partner

He says I'm writing him out of it all—
the phone ringing, the collage making,
the constant recitation of my speech
in our spare room. He's writing about this
now because it's strange, he says,
to be erased. But I knew he was there,
just like I was there, just like oxygen
was there. Something implicit, unwavering,
like a break against the shore.

The Easter After

My hands are full of Tesco chocolate eggs,
thin straws from colored baskets.

I want to resurrect you. Need to remember
the soft details of it all.

People move around me,
lumber trolleys down the aisles

as I drown in watery dyes, the taste
of dark yolks, bottles of milk for Charlene.

Those were the days you tried to do it right—
drink less, yell quieter, hit softer—

give us the sweet things
that you never had.

Still talking

The night I sat on the couch,
heard Mom cry down the phone
from thousands of miles away,
otherwordly heaving, signal
fading, you were dead:
I split like atoms.

A part of me forever left
in a time when you still moved,
called me honey, sent pictures
of your dog.

Another thrust forward
into a world where talking to you
through poetry is sad. Our memories
are not for dwelling.

Buck up, they say here,
buck up.

Other versions

I see men in the street
about your age and want to
run to them

                to smell their leather jackets,
                examine their tattoos, hear stories
                about what life was like in prison.

I want to touch
their bristly faces
but I don't.

                They are not you

and I must move on
to better men.

Purpose

Pigeons move like addicts
through bins,
scuffling.

Crowd together
in chaotic formations,
knowing

at any point
they may be kicked
or shooed away.

These are city birds,
not used to flying
or settling down

without their manic pecking,
they would have
nothing else

to do.

Connection

My grandmother-in-law is dying.

She doesn't remember me often
but likes that I'm American—
calls me a 'Yank' in her London accent
and sneaks me Baileys every Christmas,
even though I'm old enough to drink.

I watch her daughter, retired now,
sitting by the hospital bed.
I understand this: the worry,
the waiting.

But I understand too
that I am cracked clay,
a lightless lamp, a blind bird.
I cannot do anything.

Her grief ebbs forward, fills the room.
My eyes dart, palms clench the edges
of the chair as I will the tea to come,
so I can turn away and forget
where we are.

Endings

She called it a circus,
the death of her mother.
It happened over days
in a village home filled
with family, tired of travelling.

She always imagined the death
would be dignified, not full
of noise, lost keys, morphine drips
and too many trips to the pub.
It was not what she expected.

And yet, I can't help but wonder
if you would have preferred that,
a scene from a dark comedic play,
to your quiet dirty death,
slipping away unnoticed
like hair down a drain.

Marching on

The first funeral
after your funeral
went better than expected.
I didn't cry out, didn't accuse
everyone in the church
of not knowing pain, the hot
ooze of an addict's death.
Instead I listened to the click
of heels on pavement, the measured
warm-feeling speeches, the march
of an expensive casket, and knew
that with every funeral I attended
yours would become less significant,
the fading page of a psalm in my room.

Lesson #7

She told me it felt like peeing
but nicer when a man
did it right, after marriage.
Until then you must hide
it away, she said, keep it
glowing, like a firefly
caught in a jar.

Looming

Next week will be one year
since you died. I wait for it,
stay awake at night considering
what I will do to commemorate the day:
wake up, eat Muesli, bathe,
post on Facebook. I imagine
the morning and the afternoon
but not the night, and never
the day after. Those are coming
for me, like a hunter
tracking a fawn.

Conscientious

He showed me the files
before he left for China—
blue for the house, red for the bills,
yellow for me. He remembered
how long it took to sift through
the folded papers and receipts
stuffed into the crumbling drawers
of your house. If I die, he said,
I want it to be easier
on you.

Now

I cry all the time
in the most inappropriate places,
even when I don't feel sad.
My eyes leak like gasoline
from the fuel pump
you masking-taped together
in my old Granada,
or like the patio roof
you never managed to patch up
before the fire.

My body knows you're dead.

No matter how much I know
I should not be crying
in a toilet cubicle,
in my office,
on the street when I see
people holding hands,
my body remembers
you, in the fat salty tears
which well up and spill
out, just like your laugh
when you were alive.

Lesson #8

Shortly after I told him
that he should stay home more
he pulled up in the drive,
a big screen TV strapped
to the back of his pickup.
Now, he said puffing out his chest,
you'll never be lonely again.

When you sneak up on me

It's nearly your birthday again
and I feel like throwing up—
feel the bile from sweet meats
and mince pies rising, the sickly
turn of my stomach. I thought
I was done with this— believed
it would just be tears from now on,
not the long nights begging
for sleep, the searing headaches,
the terrible fear I will lose
all the things I love.
But worst of all, I thought
the anxiety was over,
the sensation of being stalked
by someone I trusted.

Echo

The FedEx envelope thuds
through the door like lead,
sits unopened on the table
for days: I know what this means.

Everything is paid now:
your back taxes, medical bills,
the air conditioner
in your house.

Your name will no longer pop up
on computer screens in Florida offices.
Strangers will not think about you anymore.

What you have left is now archived
or in the hands of your relatives
who have already stopped
talking about you.

I want to scream—
let the debt collectors keep seeking,
let them keep asking for you, by name,
let someone, besides me,
keep calling after you.

Dry

I am running out of things
to say about you.
Blame me for your second death.

Two Years

I have never wanted to be alone
more than I do right now,
to block the sounds outside
from seeping in—
children rolling scooters
the *slap slap* of laundry
being pinned to a line,
footsteps on floorboards upstairs.

Everything inside me rushes, rages
against the noise, the persistent presence
of people, cats, birds, televisions
all existing when really,

only you should exist today,
on the anniversary of your death

the day when you began pressing me

down,
        down,
                down

until I sit here hating all the things
I used to love.

Lesson #9

He told me after I blew out
the candles on my cake
that I better marry quickly.
My hair and hips were good
and I would need the money
more than I'd ever need the love.

The Academic

I am giving a presentation
and wonder if it's disrespectful
to include your photo
in my Powerpoint.

I remember when it was taken—
how you checked the mirror,
pulled the plastic comb
from your back pocket and swept
it through your hair three times,
like always, then stole another glance
before the click of the camera.

I decide to put the photo in—
you looked good that day
and I know how you loved
the attention of strangers.

What grief has become

When I think of you I'm sad—
not lonely or regretful or guilty,
just sad. That bottom-line emotion
that tells me something's wrong,
something's missing.

I would have called you today
to talk about my dress,
my Welsh and rustic wedding.
You always said I should get married,
shouldn't waste my hips.

I know you would have listened too
told me it was great,
called me some sweet name
before you put down the phone
when the neighbors came in.

I am sad we'll never do this again.

Never talk in conversational code,
me calling you, you listening to me
both of us pretending I'm not ringing
so early just to hear your voice
before it starts to slur.

On making life change

I could let it take over again:
the pulsing tiredness, the stress,
the heavier body that came from
grieving for you. But instead
I walk— in a yellow dress
bought from the home country—
straight into fear, holding
a compass, to make sure
I know my way.

On learning to help myself

I am lucky
my legs did not break
when I leapt with a collapsible umbrella
two stories from our roof.

I am lucky
the flood water surrounding
our car when I was eleven only seeped up
to my chest and no farther.

I am lucky
my skull did not split open
the day I was thrown onto the rock pile
from atop our race track stallion.

I am lucky
when my brother pushed
your hunting arrow into my love handle
it did not reach my appendix.

Finally, I am lucky
that addiction hasn't claimed me
so I can go on living without
having to rely

on luck.

Because

I know you are dead
I hold my breath whenever
I make lasagna, when my boss pats me
on the back, when I see little girls
eating ice cream in Bute Park.

Because I know you are dead
I insist on keeping my last name
after marriage, and now am
considering having kids of my own, so,
perhaps, I can see
your blue eyes again.

Because I know you are dead
my body wants sleep, has stretched
and marked itself with purple lines
after too-many late nights
and drinks in the house alone.

Because I know you are dead, I fear
all the men in my life will soon
be sad or will die
or both.

Your estate has closed

but I know you wanted
to be so much more
than ink on a page,
ashes in my closet.

One day your memory
will shrink to the head of a pin
and we will all go on—
everything you were
will die with us.

Lesson #10

He told me, slurring,
the last time we spoke
that women could never
be trusted, called them
names I'd rather not repeat,
then said that he loved me
anyway, that he was proud
of who I had become.

Recognition

The woman in Burger King shouts—
she wants fries but has no money.
Her nostrils flare, full of blood,
her eyes won't focus,
people move away.

I imagine you did this too,
at your worst.

I wonder if this woman is a mother,
if some morning she'll remember
a small moment when she chased
seagulls with her daughter,
laughed at cartoons with her son.

No one thinks about this now
as they step aside, pretending
not to look.

Resilience

Shuddering I walk past it,
the dead pigeon on my way to work
always in the same position
but each day with fewer feathers,
less organs, more leaves.

Even though it upsets me
and there are more pleasant ways
to go – I still choose this path,
still slow down and look directly
at the bird's soft, open body,

force myself to internalize the loss,
hoping that one day
I'll accept it.

Finding You

Covered in tick bites and sweat
I found my way to the music store
you'd talked about. The man behind
the counter knew your name, and mine,
shook his head when I told him the news,
such a shame, he said. Then I realized it,

this had been your place,

not the flea-infested house or the beaches
full of needles. Not the bloated body
on the bed.

I had found you, here.

When the man brought out the guitar,
I cried more than I ever have in public.
He said you came in every day
for two months before you chose
the perfect one, for me.

Notes

'Men in Our Family Die Early':

The word 'cur' refers to an 'aggressive or unkempt dog, especially a mongrel' as well as 'a contemptible man'. In North America, this word can also be used to elicit pity or demonstrate that something is both a predator and a victim.

'Guide':

The word 'realtor' is used in North America as a shortened version of 'real estate agent', someone who is licensed to negotiate and arrange real estate sales.

Source: Oxford English Dictionary. (2017). [online] Oed.com. Available at: http://www.oed.com/

Acknowledgements

Acknowledgements are due to the editors of *Bare Fiction Magazine*, *Meniscus*, *The Fem Lit Mag*, *The Lonely Crowd*, *Acumen*, *The Interpreter's House* and *Cheval 9* where versions of these poems were first published.

I would also like to thank those who have encouraged me along this challenging but important journey. Thank you to all the poets I have met and worked with over the years for your inspiration as well as to the friends and family who extended their love and support from around the globe after the death of my father. There are far too many to list here but you know who you are.

In particular, I am grateful to Sara, Tom, Renn, Emma, and Charlotte who have let me talk endlessly about death and poetry. I am indebted to my supervisor, colleague and friend, Richard Gwyn, whose skillful and compassionate guidance has helped to shape me and my work. I would also like to thank my talented editor, Susie Wild, whose thoughtfulness and creativity led the poems to a place they needed to go.

Finally, I owe enormous thanks to my husband, Richard Daly, who has read and re-read everything more times than I can count. His steadfast love and beautiful meals nourished me through one of the darkest times in my life and, ultimately, gave me the support I needed to produce this collection.